Welcoming Asylum Seekers

Struggles and Joys in the Local Church

Stephen Burns

Tutor in Liturgy at the Queen's Foundation
for Ecumenical Theological Education, Birmingham

GROVE BOOKS LIMITED
RIDLEY HALL RD CAMBRIDGE CB3 9HU

Contents

Acknowledgments
Thank you to Eveline Carr, Steve Croft, Di Johnson, Gavin Wakefield and Jon Wilkinson, my colleagues in Gateshead and the UMC, who helped me to flourish.

The Cover Illustration is by Peter Ashton

First Impression April 2004
ISSN 1470-854X
ISBN 1 85174 560 2

Thinking in Context 1

This booklet reflects my experience of parish ministry as large numbers of asylum seekers and refugees began to settle in the local community where I worked and lived.

To me at least their arrival was unexpected and, as far as I know, the fact that thousands of them would make homes in the locality had not been well-publicized—perhaps for obvious reasons. Yet these new groups came to have a most significant impact on the local community, upon the church and upon the shape of my ministry. The arrival of asylum seekers presented a number of serious challenges and invited some wonderful encounters. Asylum seekers are too often considered to be primarily a problem—and the problems are indeed often manifold—but my title for this booklet, echoing as it does Hebrews 13.2, and much of the tone of my reflections, is intended to combat the commonplace focus on the problematic and instead properly to celebrate what the presence of asylum seekers may come to mean. At the same time, I shall explore some of the complexities to which 'struggle' in my subtitle alludes.

We shall explore some of the complexities to which 'struggle' in my subtitle alludes

In what follows I have adopted a narrative style. I introduce the experience of some of those I met, discuss some of my own experience of working with asylum seekers and refugees, and explore some theological and biblical resources for upholding this kind of ministry. I had originally intended to include an overview or survey of government policy relating to asylum. But this has proved to be impossible, as asylum law and practice are so quickly changing, rapidly out of date and thoroughly confusing. The booklet therefore finds a narrower focus on the pastoral and theological dimensions of a particular experience.[1] I hope it will be encouraging and useful to other congregations in their own attempts to welcome strangers and at the end of the booklet I have suggested some questions to consider in forming a response to the issues I introduce.[2]

A Geography of Division

The parish to which I have referred is Gateshead.[3] It is the northern-most point in the diocese of Durham, and is separated from the neighbouring diocese of Newcastle by the river Tyne. Very little contact was made or sustained between the neighbouring parishes that fell on either side of the diocesan boundaries. This is notable not least because increasingly and in various ways the identities of Gateshead and Newcastle were being fused together, especially through a joint bid as 'Newcastle-Gateshead' to be a contender for European City of Culture status in 2008. The bid failed but its very existence indicated the significant amount of regeneration that was (and still is) taking place.[4] Much of this development is centred around the banks of the Tyne, and most of the regeneration to date has been largely arts-based and arts-led: the BALTIC is a converted mill and now Britain's second contemporary art gallery, after Tate Modern. It stands next to the almost completed Sage Music Centre, a mammoth yet gracious building with a gentle resemblance to Sydney's Opera House. Its shape consciously recalls the way in which the Sydney Harbour Bridge was modelled on the Tyne Bridge. The Tyne also has a new bridge of its own, the Gateshead Millennium Bridge. These three projects represent the investment of millions of pounds in the local region, and they became possible in large part following the success of Gateshead Council a few years earlier in commissioning the Angel of the North. This, Britain's largest piece of public sculpture, stands on space at the south of the town, alongside the A1 trunk road. It was the result of an arts project, proposed as a solution to prevent mine workings damaging the road. The Angel is embedded in the mine, which was filled with concrete to hold the structure above ground.[5]

> *It is notable that it has been largely the case that asylum seekers have been placed in severely deprived communities*

These arts-led regeneration initiatives invite the possibility of reversing some of Gateshead's fortunes. The town is perhaps best known for its longstanding and widespread social deprivation, captured in the moniker that it is 'the dirty back lane to Newcastle,' and reaffirmed in the 2000 publication of the then Department of Environment, Transport and the Regions, *Indices of Deprivation*, which situated central Gateshead (Bede ward) as the 117th most deprived ward of the 8,414 in Britain. It is notable that it has been largely the case that asylum seekers have been placed in severely deprived communities.

Communities like Gateshead were very much the focus of the Church of England's mid-1980s document, *Faith in the City*,[6] which explored the plight of spatial casualties of urbanization, those parts of cities and urban environ-

4

ments in which social disintegration had become most acute. These urban areas are the focus of a range of difficult problems, sometimes referred to as an 'anatomy of deprivation'—dereliction, delinquency, segregation, unemployment, poor services, low pay, ill-health, poor housing, stigmatization, vandalism—each of which spiral out from the key problems of poverty and crime.[7] Significantly, Christian reflection on such spatial areas has come to focus on the 'faces' in this anatomy—segregated *people*, delinquent *children*, the derelict *human* environment, and so on.[8] In Gateshead, asylum seekers certainly came to be significant faces in the anatomy of deprivation.

The sense conveyed by longer-term locals was of 'invasion' on all sides

The arrival of asylum seekers at the same time as areas of the town were being regenerated left many of the longer-term local people experiencing a deep sense of disorientation. On the one hand, new people were moving into the community through association with the regeneration projects. A flurry of luxury apartments were built to attract them, introducing a housing stock very different from the majority of homes in the town. On the other hand, asylum seekers were being moved into some of the very worst of the generally poor housing. The sense conveyed by longer-term locals was of invasion on all sides.

Urban Mission

Another important feature of my particular experience was the link between the parish and the nearby Anglican theological college, Cranmer Hall, situated in Durham some fourteen miles to the south. Ministry among asylum seekers was possible in Gateshead only because of our connection with Cranmer. The 'Urban Mission Centre' was the project bridging the two, and had been operational, though in different forms, since the mid-1980s. The purpose of the UMC was to provide a setting for students to learn the dynamics of contextual theology, and to facilitate contact with people affected by the issues that gathered together in particular kinds of deprived urban contexts. The relationship between college and the local church was fruitful and much was made possible in the parish by the constant stream of enthusiasm and dedication from students together with the careful oversight of the project by staff. Over time as vicar, however, a number of downsides to the UMC became apparent to me, despite its many strengths. At the heart of the ambiguity was the way that the ministries of the local church people may have been substituted by the students' ministries, perhaps even allowing the local church to evade its own responsibilities for mission and ministry. Certainly, among asylum seekers, student presence emphasised and reinforced local reserve about engaging with these newcomers.

Undergirding my belief that the UMC should be reconceived in ways more likely to avoid the pitfall of substituting local ministries was my sense of the need for the urban mission project to engage with some larger challenges in the area of urban mission. These had emerged as a critique of traditional Anglican 'consensus' models of urban mission (including *Faith in the City*).[9]

What this critique might mean for ministry among asylum seekers raises many controversial questions, and ones which local churches in Gateshead addressed quite differently in the range of responses to asylum seekers which they adopted.

A World of Faiths

The was a third feature of great significance in our context. Gateshead is home to one of the largest Hasidic Jewish communities outside Israel. Long before the advent of latter-day asylum seekers, Gateshead had a fascinating history of sanctuary and immigration. Documentary evidence about the local Hasidic community suggests that from its origins in the late nineteenth century (when a number of families migrated south of the Tyne after a schism from Newcastle's Orthodox Jewish community) until the years leading up to the Second World War, the Jewish residents of Gateshead had enjoyed a considerable amount of integration in the wider community. This changed in the years following the Second World War when the Gateshead Jewish community grew considerably in number and so more self-sufficient and less dependant on the wider community. As a result it became increasingly separate. The whole religious scene locally, which comprised several other faith groups (and which, with the exception of the Jewish community, constituted a very active Interfaith Forum) was dominated by the Jewish community. It is notable that the numbers and the visibility of believing, worshipping and belonging members[10] of the Hasidic Jews significantly overshadowed the number of Christians who would fit the definition of believing, worshipping and belonging—or indeed of Christians alongside committed members of the range of other faiths represented locally.

In the story of the Hasidic community, there was a legacy in living memory of separate incoming communities in Gateshead

In the story of the Hasidic community, there was a legacy in living memory of separate incoming communities in Gateshead, and this was underlined by the concentration of Jewish homes in the area around the local synagogue. This constituted a visibly different and, though international, culturally homogenous community which arguably invited a particular mindset towards incoming peoples at a later stage. Significantly, the Home Office had tendered a large share of its provision for asylum seekers to a local Jewish company of landlords.

Of course, every context is different, and perhaps few direct parallels can be drawn with other places. What this section is intended to highlight is that context is highly determinative of response at many levels.

Context is highly determinative of response at many levels

2

My own first encounter with an asylum seeker locally was in fact at the nearby city of Sunderland.

On learning that Gateshead was to 'receive' asylum seekers, I decided to visit a project that was in the process of being established in Sunderland, in order to see how we in Gateshead might follow its lead and learn from its lessons.

When I arrived, I encountered a group of perhaps a dozen men, all of whom were separated from their families. They were of different ages, and some of them were pining for wives and children, others for parents and brothers and sisters. I discovered that they held within their group a remarkable mix of skills, many of them being highly educated or highly skilled. All of our conversation took place through an interpreter with whom they had come to meet at the church hall, their primary aim being to improve their grasp of the English language.

For all of the men, simply getting to this gathering had proved difficult

It transpired that for all of the men, the experience simply of getting to this gathering had proved difficult. Only some were in possession of the bus pass to which they were entitled. Not all of those had had the pass explained to them in a way that they could understand, and so they had been unable to use it, not being able to communicate in English. One man told me that he had been in Sunderland for almost six weeks and had been coaxed out of his hostel for the first time today; he had simply been so overwhelmed by a strange city, with its strange climate, full of strangers. Some of the men, a group of Iraqis, told me that they had been housed in a hostel with another group of men, Iranians of similar ages—this seemed an extraordinary rooming arrangement given their shared history of the Iran-Iraq war.

This situates interfaith dialogue and fellowship at the forefront of issues relating to hospitality to asylum seekers

On my visit, a church group brought a spread of sandwiches to eat—a generous gesture, except that the sandwiches had been made up with ham, and so proved unintentionally offensive to this group of largely Muslim men. A related story demonstrates a similar *faux pas*—local Christians had offered furnishings to brighten emergency accommodation for asylum seekers, yet pictures and wall-hangings depicting the human form had proved offensive to their Muslim recipients, despite all good intentions. Incidents of this kind alert Christians to their need to learn of other people's faith and traditions; this means that engagement in interfaith dialogue is an indispensable part of being ready to offer hospitality to asylum seekers.

Yet despite these difficulties of which I learned, I had within weeks both heard about and witnessed extraordinary kindness towards asylum seekers on the part of local Christians and others. For instance, a school class of ten-year-olds had welcomed a Kosovan student into their midst by all learning to welcome and encourage her, and introduce themselves in her mother tongue. This notwithstanding, my overall impression after several meetings with asylum seekers was of their immense vulnerability, and of deep trauma arising from the fear and violence to which they testified.

My overall impression after several meetings with asylum seekers was of their immense vulnerability

What I encountered in this regard seems to be by no means isolated. The first testimony of *Changing Lives—Stories of Exile*, a publication of the British Refugee Council, begins: 'I fled from my native land because of the danger I was in...' The theme is echoed throughout: 'I had two probabilities, they would kill me or I should go...'; 'they took our freedom from us'; 'there was shooting and killing all around.'[11] Several publications of the Refugee Council similarly present the first-hand testimony of refugees, some of them gathering together stories from a particular exodus. One such publication is *My Name Came Up: Kosovo—War, Exile and Return*. Published in 2000, it is able to convey both the traumas of leaving and also the first thoughts of some of those who returned to their homeland after finding temporary sanctuary in the UK. The narratives of Kosovans' time in Britain echoes much of what I heard at first hand in Gateshead, many Kosovans being among the asylum seekers I encountered. Many of the testimonies in *My Name Came Up* illustrate both the problems faced by asylum seekers and the startling generosity they also sometimes met, just as I had encountered. An extract from the story of Selvete and her children, then living in Leeds, is called 'I will always be your child,' and it conveys well something of both trauma and generosity:

Selvete and her children are showing signs of recovery in a city that she says has been 'fantastic' to her. 'No-one has said a bad word to me.' In Leeds, local school children collected toys among themselves and delivered them to Brakenhurst Reception Centre in the days after the refugees arrived. 'I can't explain to you how it felt when we finally arrived at the airport in Leeds,' continues Selvete. 'To see all those people standing there waiting to take care of us. I was so ashamed in our dirty clothes. We weren't looking our best, but they kept telling us it didn't matter.'

Selvete says Alberta [her daughter] has taken to behaving like a mother herself. 'When I cry, she says to me, "Mummy, what is it, why are you crying?" And then she recites her list: "Is it because the house was burnt? Is it because Uncle Mome got killed? Is it because Daddy is not here?"...[12]

For those who have not heard such testimony for themselves, another powerful but disturbing means of hearing the echoes of some of these sentiments is to see Michael Winterbottom's recent film, *In This World*. It depicts the journey of two young Afghani refugees, Jamal and Enayatulla, as they travel from a Pershewer refugee camp to London. En route, they travel through Pakistan, Iran, Turkey, and Italy, all the time vulnerable to people smugglers and racketeers. On one occasion they are turned back by border guards, to begin again, the money they had paid for their transportation gone and irrecoverable. They find themselves stealing away on cargo vessels, sleeping in squalor, working in sweat shops, hungry and cold. In Italy, they are sealed in a cargo container along with a couple and their newborn baby, with no idea of how long the sea-route to the UK may take. All but the newborn and Jamal, the youngest of the two Iraqis, die of asphyxiation, unable to break free from the metal box in which they are enclosed. The title of the film, *In This World*, echoes Jamal's telephone call from London to his family in Pershewer: 'Enayatulla is not in this world.'

Preaching and Celebrating the Gospel

3

Following my visit to Sunderland, and on hearing stories of exile for myself, I began to preach about what I was learning about asylum as a way of preparing the congregation to face those who would become our new neighbours.

My own key questions were about how attention to Scripture might engender empathy that would lead to action in the congregation.

Given the social context of Gateshead (outlined in chapter one), a comment from a daily newspaper just before my first sermon on the subject impressed the importance of preparing the community. A cleric in London was reporting his own experience of working to welcome asylum seekers to his community, and noted the difficulty of engaging the congregation and other local people. The phrase he used was that they themselves so often felt 'overlooked,' and so might especially struggle to see others 'overtake' them in line for benefit. This sense was especially present in Gateshead given that it was not just those with nothing, arriving as asylum seekers, who were felt to destabilize the local community—there were also the rich associated with the regeneration. This sense of 'threat' among the longstanding local community was something that would need to be explored in relation to Scripture.

This sense of 'threat' was something that would need to be explored in relation to Scripture

Opening the Scriptures

Initially a sermon series about asylum seekers took place through a stretch of ordinary time leading up to Advent. Two scriptural themes seemed to suggest themselves for a local lectionary: the narrative of Jesus' own exile into Egypt; and the notion of the communion of saints with its focal image of 'citizens of heaven.'[13] The story of Jesus' own exile involves concrete imagery, meshes with widespread concern for the care of children, and might provide a strong basis for empathy and solidarity with contemporary exiles. The theme of the communion of saints was already important for us as it directly related to the departed loved ones of a largely elderly congregation.

One of the most challenging resources for reflection on the gospel traditions of the 'flight into Egypt' (Matthew 2.13–18) is the commentary on this text emerging from marginalized groups, such as those whose voices are amplified by liberation theologians. Approaching the text through the lens of liberation theology at least sidesteps some of the preoccupation in Western commentary with the narrative's setting in the highly mythological context of the canonical birth narratives, which whilst doubtless important, may not so readily yield insight that maps onto the experience of those in 'flight' to the West, and elsewhere, today. 'Liberation exegesis' is itself a controversial notion, at least among Western academics who underline its vulnerability to 'eisegesis'—reading our concerns into the text. In our context, it may be precisely this vulnerability that is its chief merit. Consider the Bible study on the 'flight' to which *The Gospel in Art by the Peasants of Solentiname* bears witness. Gathered for Bible study on the readings for Sunday mass, Fernando, a Jesuit priest, relates to his Nicaraguan parishioners:

> How often have I read that Saint Joseph and the Virgin fled to Egypt. But only now, when an army patrol has just come, have I really understood that very real and harsh circumstance that the gospel presents to us here: repression. We can imagine what that means: leaving at night, hiding with great fear, leaving everything behind, and having to reach the border because they are being pursued.[14]

The text is vivified by the contemporary connections that the priest is able to make. In the unfolding conversation, others join Father Fernando in relating the text to their time and place—the *campesino* families forced to leave home, fleeing misery, forced from their land, victimized by the National Guard. Ernesto, a parishioner, directly relates the Scriptures to what he has seen and heard for himself: 'the picture of all those families fleeing, mothers carrying their children in their arms, is the same as the flight into Egypt.' Others in the group follow Ernesto's lead and associate the persecution of 'stunted, undernourished' Nicaraguan children with the persecution of Christ. The readers' own children and the young of their land are like Christ because they 'have had the rich against them' since they were 'at [the] mother's breast.' And their Bible study leads to associations with other Scriptures, so the *Magnificat* comes to mind. Christ's persecution, from the flight to the cross, is seen as a consequence of the contest set up in Mary's song: 'he will cast down the mighty from their thrones and lift up the lowly' (Luke 1.52–53). Aligning themselves and their children with Christ, and Somoza's National Guard with Herod, the Bible readers conclude that 'the business of Herod and Christ is what we have right here,' 'what we're seeing is the living story of the life of Jesus.'[15]

Of obvious importance in the *The Gospel in Art* is the image that accompanies this commentary. It bolsters the contemporary connections related in the 'peasant's' comments. It is especially important to note that in our own reading of the biblical text and this commentary in Gateshead, the related image in *The Gospel in Art* was fundamental to our appropriation of Scripture. For Gateshead is a context in which many people struggle with text, quite possibly being unable to read and likely to fit Unlock's description of 'those who can read, but don't.'[16] Image was, as always, a crucial tool for approaching the story, beginning to open up understanding of it, and encouraging a handling of it that related to our own present circumstances. Miriam Guevara's image of the flight in *The Gospel in Art* depicts a suckling mother, riding a donkey, accompanied by a man on

Image was a crucial tool for approaching the story

foot, as they pass through a lush forest full of bright vegetation and wildlife. This is not the near-east, but the Nicaraguan readers' own land. And the figures of the holy family are not Mediterranean (and even less so 'stained-glass' white), but Latino, dressed in the working clothes of the *campesino*.

Complementary Insights

Other commentaries provide insights that complement this particular approach to the story of the flight. The reason for the flight being the 'massacre of the innocents' maps the baby as the new Moses, echoing the traditions of Exodus (1.15–22), heightening readers' anticipation of the significance of Jesus. For instance, this point is picked up directly in *Just Jesus: The Passion Book*, the third in José Ignacio López Vigil and Maria López Vigil's journalistic representation of the gospel from a Latin American perspective. They imagine a character encouraging Joseph:

> Going away doesn't mean letting yourself die. Look at Moses: he, too, was an exile, but later on, he returned. Therefore, if one goes away, he [sic] brings with him the hope of coming back.[17]

Despite inviting type and allegory of the kind the *Just Jesus* character reflects, there are also some deeply historical trends embedded in the biblical story. Emerging from an era of Jewish diaspora, the Matthean infancy narrative clusters a number of features which reflect the commonplace experience of exile and immigration. This was focused, as in the scriptural tradition, on Egypt, and especially the northern cities of Elephantine and Alexandria, effectively Jewish colonies at the time of Herod. The stories of the magi, of the massacre of the innocents, and of the flight into Egypt, each in their own and related ways, acknowledge and engage with this context.

The biblical stories also present in powerful ways some of the thematic heart of the canonical gospels, relating Christ's experience to his later teaching and practice. When the López Vigils' comment on their journalistic representation of the gospel witness, they emphasize 'love without boundaries' as the essence of the gospel, and they see the flight as leading into this theme. Exile may engender a sense that all just persons are compatriots, they suggest.[18] Whilst 'love without boundaries' resonates with much of what the canonical Christ preaches and practises (at table, in particular), the biblical narrative of the flight into Egypt also invites some serious questions which should not be overlooked. These relate to the heart of the gospel, in so far as they focus on the ambiguous image of God presented by the story, which its miraculous aspects magnify. The birth of Jesus is ascribed to divine action, epiphany and intervention characterize the events at Bethlehem, and then the flight invites jarring questions about divine activity as it seems that 'God saved his own son but left the other children to die.'[19] And it is not that God is bracketed-out of the flight whilst present otherwise, but rather that God is present, puzzlingly warning just one family—'his own'—of the imminent massacre. The force of the problem may explain in part many interpreters' preference for mythological designations for the infancy narratives as a genre. The sense of 'unfairness' and its invitation to question God's own morality was not lost in Gateshead.[20]

Celebrating Christmas

The force of the flight narrative, in both its palatable and unpalatable aspects, may be especially difficult to hear in the context of a contemporary Christmas. This is for different reasons: on the one hand, the ambiguous image of the divine grates against sentimental representations of God present in at least parts of popular culture, and to which the legacy of Victorian Christmases may be particularly hospitable. On the other hand, the consumerism inherent in contemporary Christmases disenfranchises those in need rather than plenty. Even if we concede that the Christian tradition no longer determines 'the meaning of Christmas' for many people in the West, it seems to me that the emergence of asylum seekers in the community calls for the retrieval of Christmastide, the Christmas season, in the local church, in order to relate the gospel to their particular contemporary needs. How might patterns for worship encourage the task of welcoming strangers?

The story of the flight has an important place in the liturgical celebration of Christmastide, being commemorated on December 28, the third feast in a

The flight narrative may be especially difficult to hear in the context of a contemporary Christmas

series comprised of Stephen (December 26) and John (December 27). Together these feasts were ascribed in the Middle Ages as celebrations of the 'Companions of Christ,' understood to mark three types of martyrdom.[21] The Commemoration of Holy Innocents involved some other fascinating medieval developments that amplify some of the subversions that come to the fore in the biblical narratives. These included the practice of upturning the liturgical hierarchy for the day, with bishops and priests relegated to the choir, and choirboys acting in primary liturgical roles, and sometimes preaching. As in the stable, children became the focus; and echoing the *Magnificat*, the lowly were lifted up to places of honour.[22] In the case of these liturgical celebrations, the subversions were temporary, of course. But they signal some grasp of the dynamics of divine activity in incarnation.

Traditions Old and New

Yet dynamics of this kind are almost entirely obscured by contemporary celebrations of Christmas, in which the darkness of Advent is also obscured by the 'stretching' of Christmas earlier into December, in which sentimental carols predominate,[23] and which may now in many places—Gateshead among them—centre on Christingle as the best attended celebration not only of Christmas but of the whole year. Notwithstanding the evangelistic potential of the Christingle service, it is especially vulnerable to some of the limits of the modern Christmas. Christingle (in notable contrast to the Commemoration of Holy Innocents which dates from around 505CE) is a relatively recent addition to the church's repertoire, involving hand-held symbols: an orange to represent the world, four sticks of fruit or sweets to represent the 'four corners' and 'four seasons' of the earth, red ribbon to represent the blood of Christ, and a lighted candle to represent Christ's appearance. Although employing the traditional (northern hemisphere) seasonal imagery of light and darkness to powerful effect, often in practice the Christingle service seems in its 'explanation' of the meaning of the images it employs to invite prescribed and predictable interpretations that mute some of the challenging aspects of biblical Christmas narratives. Making Christingle unfold as a disaster which brings unexpected blessing ('euchatastrophy', in Mary Collins' helpful term[24]) seems a long way away from most actual Christingle presentations. In the Christingle, red ribbon may intend to point towards 'the blood of Christ', but if it does so in a context which has to a great extent long lost use of such imagery,[25] it is likely to do so in an altogether less disturbing way than the memory of Jesus' suffering enacted in bread being broken and wine poured out in the setting of a narrative of 'betrayal' by 'night' (compare 1 Corinthians 11.23). Yet it is exactly exposure to the Bible's sense of realism about the latter that may be needed if strangers are to be welcomed empathically.

Celebration and Response

It is a pity, then, that the tradition of Las Posadas, which originated in Latin America but has spread to the North, has not been popularized in Britain as it has elsewhere, for this may better relate the shadows in the Christmas narratives and so encourage resistance to sentimentalizing of the tradition. It is a way of celebrating the gospel that invites response to contemporary asylum seekers. Congenially for celebrants of Christmas which is focused on December 25, it also concentrates on the gospel lectionary for the principal service of the day itself (Luke 2.1–20).

In the Las Posadas, miniature figures of the holy family are 'housed' at the homes of various parishioners through the Advent season, and then are eventually brought to the gathered church community for a service on Christmas Eve, the time at which Christingle is most popular. The ritual of movement from one home to another of course represents the holy family's journey to Bethlehem according to biblical tradition, and the liturgical text which accompanies the rite of welcome and departure at each home, as well as the culminating Christmas Eve finale, incorporates a strong sense of the desperation of the family in their vulnerable state, with obvious resonance with the plight of contemporary refugees. Fragments of dialogue include, on the lips of Mary and Joseph: 'we are tired and we are cold. May we please have shelter?...It is not by our own choice that we travel...' And from the mouths of those who refuse them, 'You look dirty and you smell...for your kind there is no place, our inn is decent...For your reasons we care not, every room is taken...you are bad for business.'[26] Housed in people's homes, perhaps amidst children's fashion and action toys—Barbie, Action Man and such like—euchatastrophic realities may be vividly explored in this ritual.

The liturgical text incorporates a strong sense of the desperation of the family in their vulnerable state

Within the scriptural narrative of the flight into Egypt, and in the liturgical celebration of the Christmas season, I believe that there is good news for asylum seekers, and rich resources for Christian people who seek to welcome strangers.

Welcoming Strangers: Galvanizing Practical Action

4

As Gateshead approached the task of welcoming strangers, many Christian communities in the north-east as a whole were also galvanizing practical action among asylum seekers.

Much of it was much more extensive and impressive than that which emerged in Gateshead. In this chapter, I explore further some of the complexities of our own situation. We began to recognise the plight of contemporaries in flight and the resources we drew on in Scripture and tradition engendered solidarity with them in their need. But this by no means translated easily into practical action. The Gateshead Christian community's 'performance' of the Scriptures[27] of Christmastide was always stumbling.

As mentioned in the earlier chapter 'Thinking in Context,' students from Cranmer Hall were central to what was possible. Visiting, translating, support in teaching and hospitality were just some of the things that students offered. A constant frustration was, however, that 'the church's work' with asylum seekers locally appeared to mean the work of the students and the clergy. A small number of church members had responded to preaching about asylum by getting involved with what began to happen; by far the vast majority did not do so. In relation to asylum seekers, as so much else, we were struggling to be the 'local, outward-looking and participative' church, as *Faith in the City* would have had us, in our urban setting.[28] In many ways, we were not local enough, for whilst not fitting the description of a 'commuter' church as is common in some suburban settings, it was nevertheless the case that many members came from beyond the parish boundaries, often exercising preferences about church style and such like. A downside of this motivation for attendance can be a weakened commitment to the geographical parish, and for us it meant that as is not uncommon in inner-city congregations, links between the church and its local geographical setting were fragile. And the Cranmer Hall students, for all their worth, were in our case a particular factor that pulled against the parish being defined by its immediate locality.

Furthermore, in a setting in which people are or feel under-resourced, the call to be outward-looking may easily seem overwhelming. Rapid social changes, few of them experienced by local people as being for the better, had perhaps eroded locals' hope about concentrating energies outwardly—for some, 'the rot had set in' to the local community, and the church was effectively a sanctuary from it. Such an approach to the church is not helped by the remnants of mythology about the Oxford Movement's contribution to the urban context, and this mythology was part of the church's memory in our context. The idea of the church as focus of the beauty of holiness arguably may, without careful caveats, be employed to discourage a sense of the holiness of engagement.

What the church often seemed to represent for its members was a sense of continuity with the past

Strange alliances between incarnational and sacramental theology were, I think, at work around the Gateshead congregation, so that a basically sacramental spirituality was not informed as it might have been by the doctrine of incarnation.[29]

Moreover, the biases of the same basically sacramental spirituality had perhaps made it difficult to take note or act upon scriptural material relevant to engagement with asylum seekers in our present time. What the church often seemed to represent for its members was a sense of continuity with the past, however tenuous. Put more positively, what was often sought from the church, and where the church was able to meet perceived needs, was in terms of providing a sense of stability. It was this that looking outwards could so readily destabilize, and which arguably was played out in efforts with asylum seekers.

In relation to this, one of the initial things I read about asylum (the newspaper article by a priest in London referred to in chapter 3, above) never lost its relevance. It highlighted how longstanding locals may themselves feel overlooked, and so may perhaps resent the attention asylum seekers receive from the council, benefits agencies, and then a church being 'outward-looking.' It is also obvious just how notoriously difficult 'participation' can be in deprived urban situations. The umbrella culture of 'benefit' militated against it in Gateshead, as just one factor in a range of social dynamics that shaped lives in diminutive ways, and encouraged passivity. It was as if a significant shift in congregational spirituality was required in order to engage in the

Sermons about asylum seekers may have at best silenced overtly racist comments

already heavily demanding environment, before welcome could be extended to asylum seekers. A renewed *sacramental* spirituality may well be what is needed, in which people come to see themselves as 'graced presences,' sacramental matter, and which helps them to relate the transformation associated with 'the body of Christ' and themselves as participants in celebration who are as much 'the body of Christ' as are bits of bread.[30] All this notwithstanding, what happened in church was, I think, that sermons about asylum seekers, even in the context of attempts to broaden out and vivify a sacramental spirituality, may have at best silenced overtly racist comments but did little to engage a sense of 'the living story of the life of Jesus,' as the Solentiname Scripture readers put it, or with a sense of selves as graced presences capable of mediating grace through offering, consecration, vulnerability and given-ness to others.[31]

Practical Action

Alongside these struggles, the students from Cranmer Hall and a very small group from the parish began some practical action with asylum seekers. A visiting scheme was set up to invite contact between the church and those arriving new to the town. Much of the contact that ensued was needs-based, and involved organizing basic provisions, helping to interpret letters and various other forms of communication to which asylum seekers were expected to respond, and facilitating access to English lessons. Some local churches with community provision were able to offer both space and staff to aid asylum seekers' learning of English. One class close to my home had, on one occasion I visited, twenty-seven first languages represented, a statistic that in itself gives a sense of the challenge of both teaching and learning in that context. Such classes could be complex for other reasons, however, particularly as asylum seekers sometimes became conscious of the problems of disclosing their national or tribal origins. Where persons had fled volatile circumstances that involved forms of tribal or national warfare, disclosure of one's allegiances, both of conviction and unchosen, could expose one to vulnerability even when thousands of miles from home. Particular sensitivities were evident around asylum seekers from regions of the former Yugoslavia, and of several turbulent African nations. It transpired in this context how, for good reason, it is often necessary for people to lie about their backgrounds. That this happens is not surprising, but it underlines the potential of even a place of 'asylum' to become deeply unsettling in a frighteningly real way.

Even a place of 'asylum' has the potential to become deeply unsettling

Visiting asylum seekers also yielded great joy. Experience of the apparently facile notion of 'the generosity of those with nothing' seemed like a reversal of the promise of Hebrews 13.2. I vividly remember the strong coffee that expressed the hospitality of a flat full of Afghani men, just as Anglo-American aggression to the Afghanistan regime was mounting. (The men had, of course, fled their homeland for their hostility—verbally or otherwise actively—to that regime). I remember the pancakes made for me by another man, who had just learned to cook since arriving in England, a necessity required since being separated from his family. Another local parish had the vision to host an event in which asylum seekers could themselves cook and host members of the local church and wider community. The possibility of this was experienced as empowering by the asylum seekers themselves, and the food was a real means to fellowship between reconfigured guests and hosts, and the evening was itself perhaps a 'foretaste of the heavenly banquet.'[32]

The evening was itself perhaps a 'foretaste of the heavenly banquet'

Dropping in to Faith

Alongside the visiting, a drop-in facility was set up. It was, I think, significant for those who attended, and gradually over time it became the focus for linking into the heart of the church's life those asylum seekers who were interested. The drop-in took place on the church's premises, therefore in the same space used for worship and fellowship on Sundays and at other times. It is easy to forget, especially perhaps in areas like Gateshead, populated predominantly by people with white skin, that many asylum seekers, despite their 'difference,' are themselves Christians. The cultural homogeneity of the local church made this point a particularly difficult thing to learn (our liturgical space with its stained-glass windows of white-skinned saints and figures of Christ compounding the problem), yet it is particularly important to impress. The drop-in involved opportunity for very simple prayer—open prayer in mother tongues, with the Lord's Prayer in unison to gather prayer together at the end. Without claiming the gift of interpretation, it was extraordinary to note just how much the meaning of prayer was conveyable in pace, tone and pitch and how joyous the glossolalic 'Our Father' could be, as if the whole world had gathered in one place. I think that if more members of the longstanding congregation had attended these prayer meetings, the church's whole approach to asylum seekers might have been transformed. They were opportunities to share in the meaning of the communion of saints.

Other liturgical foci for ministry among asylum seekers quickly emerged, though not all were as happy as the encounters just related. As news of the death of separated family members filtered through to exiles in Gateshead, markings were needed for these sad occasions. Effectively, funerals took place, but without a body, often without the presence of the other family members, and all far from the 'resting place' of the deceased. Baptisms also took place—sometimes galvanizing the hope of new beginnings for a family in a new place, both physically and metaphorically. At other times, baptisms were marked by the acute pain of the mother being separated from the child's father, a husband 'at home' and out of contact, whereabouts and state of health and mind unknown, sometimes status as living or dead beyond knowledge. It was also not unknown for baptisms to expose publicly the chaos of living precariously, perhaps with a mother not knowing whether her husband was dead or alive or ever likely to be seen again, yet pregnant by another man towards whom she has leaned in a time of acute vulnerability. What grace baptism might convey in such circumstances is unimaginable.

Worthy Reception?

Could Holy Communion convey some sense of welcoming and saving grace? As communities of asylum seekers from various parts of the world began to re-form locally, it became important to try to facilitate services in French, Spanish and other languages. Sometimes students were able to act as translators, allowing people to become more integrated in the 'host' community's

It was extraordinary to note just how much the meaning of prayer was conveyable in pace, tone and pitch

worship. Not all participants at Communion were Christians however. Not all of those who were not Christians responded agnostically to the church's hospitality. Some responded from a stance of commitment to another faith. So Muslims sometimes attended communion, their rationale being that 'Christians and Muslims both believe in one God'; Buddhists likewise, apparently appreciating a community of prayer. How in each case their participation in communion might have been rationalized is a question that was never asked, but it required some reflection on the part of the church's leaders about the traditions of Jesus' open table-fellowship as a source and inspiration for a eucharistic practice and theology which could at least be set alongside, if not contest, the emphasis on 'worthy reception' which is more central to Anglican and most other traditions.

These questions raise important related ones about evangelism. It is notable that neighbouring parishes adopted strict and vigorously enacted policies about evangelism among asylum seekers. Some positively embraced the opportunity, offering the Alpha Course to those who wished to come; others positively resisted all hints at proselytizing of these vulnerable groups. In the mêlée to respond in one way or another, my own parish simply never got round to making a decision about this matter, though I am sure it would have tended towards the latter of the two perspectives just mentioned. Nevertheless, through an open door and an open table, a small number of asylum seekers came to call themselves Christian.

These points relate somewhat uneasily to the other focus of at least my own practical action among asylum seekers arriving in Gateshead. That was the Interfaith Forum, in which I became increasingly involved. Growing up and always living in areas vastly dominated by white-skinned populations, and in a culture although secularized, occasionally conscious of a Christian back-drop, the question of relations with those of other faiths was one which I had simply never considered. I could now no longer afford the luxury of such laziness and ignorance. The question of interfaith worship never came up in the context of the forum; shared quietness for silent prayer never beckoned its participants' potential unease by use of speech, symbol or Scriptures in prayer. There may have been much wisdom in this, as it allowed the focus of the forum's work to remain on the pressing practical needs of those of minority faiths in the area. Many asylum seekers were of course committed members of other world faiths.

Whilst sermons on asylum may have silenced any explicitly racist comments in the church community, racist attack, both verbal and physical, was com-monplace in the wider community. Asylum seekers were among those subjected to the threat and reality of violence to their persons and property. The Interfaith Forum was at the heart of the endeavour to report hate crime to police and to invite police response. It was also central to attempts to gain finances to enable members of minority faiths to exercise and express their religious commitments in the local community. Advocacy with the local council was key to this, and I came to represent the various faith communities on the Local Strategic Partnership.[33] It is notable that the interfaith forum was much more active locally than the ecumenical or any denominational network of Christian churches. The issues to which the forum attended— hate, violence, crime, and so on—simply required *action*.

With an agenda like this, which was constantly pressing, the fact that the forum involved little opportunity for actual interfaith dialogue, or even lis-tening to one another's particular perspectives, may not seem surprising. It does perhaps help to explain why there was sometimes a tendency towards a kind of uncritical 'niceness' around the forum, a propensity maybe to settle on our commonalities rather than our differences in all their potential richness.[34] It also perhaps explains why on occasion latent fears of proselytization, es-pecially by Christians, sometimes surfaced. The forum was not in fact a great context for deepening our knowledge-base of the *content* of each others' faiths, and so in some measure it even permitted a continued ignorance of each other's convictions. It did, however, provide an invaluable context of friend-ship and solidarity in common purpose in which this deficit could potentially be addressed.

Fragments of Theology

In this final section, I want to identify some further theological convictions that I have come to consider to be important in approaching ministry among asylum seekers.

The first of my themes is the communion of saints. In the last chapter, I hinted at my sense of this doctrine being brought alive in the context of prayer with asylum seekers from around the world. In my second chapter, which largely focused on appropriation of Scripture, I might also have associated the communion of saints with another biblical theme that suggests itself in relation to asylum—the apostolic notion of being 'citizens of heaven' (for example Philippians 3.20) which depends in part upon a sense of being displaced in one's current circumstances. It is, however, another aspect of the communion of saints on which I wish to focus at this particular point.

In relation to situations of acute need, the doctrine is of relevance to the polity of an episcopal church—or indeed to any church which does not choose to define itself primarily in congregational terms. For it is of great importance that the wider church understands that the actual congregations that might most readily offer hospitality to strangers who happen to be asylum seekers are themselves those which are already most over-

In relation to situations of acute need, the doctrine is of relevance to the polity of an episcopal church

stretched. They are likely to be churches in areas in which forms of socio-economic deprivation are already entrenched, and which are perhaps heavily burdened by the multiple pressures of their difficult context. The notion of the communion of saints has a role to play in animating what these smaller, stretched communities may nevertheless vitalize. As chapter one, above, made clear, students and resources from Cranmer Hall in Durham had a very real role of exactly this kind in the church's ministry among asylum seekers in Gateshead. Other Christians from other congregations also offered financial support, language skills, and other kinds of resources to the local church in Gateshead in order to enable things that would have otherwise been impossible. This was, in fact, a crucial expression of the communion of saints, a living symbol of the doctrine. Bishops and other diocesan figures have an indispensable role in exciting this kind of expression at regional level. It is much needed. And in an episcopal church, bishops may also have a further special role in engendering the solidarity of the communion of saints across the national and tribal boundaries that asylum seekers traverse.

Table Fellowship

A second theme is that of the open table fellowship of Jesus. I have alluded to this above in controversial connection to people of other faiths sharing in the Lord's Supper. Exploration of the table fellowship of Jesus raises crucial questions about authority in sacramental practice. It may also lead to an alternative vision of the church's hospitality in an era when so many congregations have imbibed the priorities of the Parish Communion Movement and so celebrate at least weekly Communion as their principal service, but have at the same time lost a sense of the wider repertoire of Christian worship. By this, I mean primarily various Services of the Word, which despite some good efforts at the level of denominational resources, have been almost entirely excluded from many churches' 'menu' of services. This is allied to the well-documented decline of the 'quiet time' and other forms of personal devotional practice. In many places, an already narrow sacramental spirituality has been shrunk down to Communion (baptism, despite some good efforts at the level of denominational resources, being sidelined out of principal services). This is relevant in underlining the key point that celebrations of Communion buoyed up by traditional Anglican and other Protestant theologies of 'worthy reception' are not an encouraging basis for hospitality to asylum seekers, or anyone else for that matter. The possibility of retrieving the traditions of Jesus' open table fellowship suggests the great promise of reconfiguring liturgical practice in a more missionary mode, and has wide application beyond the issues considered in this booklet, though I believe they are deeply relevant to them.

Various services of the word have been almost entirely excluded from many churches' 'menu' of services

The Hospitality of Jesus

The figure of Jesus is also the focus of my third and final theme. The hospitality of Jesus was the basic conviction with which I entered, despite initial reserve, into interfaith collaboration. (In the gospel story of the Syro-Phoenician woman, Jesus himself seems to model the possibility of changing one's mind about intercultural matters).[35] And Jesus himself teaches the kind of self-effacement that encourages others to seek his presence in the last and the least: 'whoever welcomes one such child in my name, welcomes me…' (Matthew 18.5); 'whatever you did for the least of these my brothers and sisters, you did for me…' (Matthew 25.40). To begin to attend to Jesus is to be invited to attend to the diverse crowd of peoples with which Jesus is concerned.[36] One contemporary Christian theologian who teaches this better than many others is Kosake Koyama, the Japanese-born missionary to Thailand, whose writings have pioneered approaches to intercultural Christology.[37] Among his remarkable writings is the encouragement to attend to people, not their 'logies':

Jesus himself teaches the kind of self-effacement that encourages others to seek his presence in the last and the least

> The seminaries did not teach me. I had to discover it by myself. They did not teach me that it is more interesting to know a Hindu than to know Hinduism; it is more rewarding to know a Buddhist than to know Buddhism, a Marxist than Marxism, a revolutionary than revolution, a missionary than missiology, wife than the 'marriage and the family' course, Jesus Christ than Christology.[38]

As Koyoma continues, 'Personal encounter (human community) is pregnant with unpredictable possibilities. The living person who confronts me defies the best possible descriptions of him.' And questions cascade from this:

> Is it perhaps possible—what a dreadful thought—that the study of theology blinded me in this respect? Has not theology inflated my language and thought? Has this inflation kept me from contact with real people?…To love them *as they are* in all their complexity and not just to love anthropological, sociological, theological 'formulations' of brothers and sisters is the command of the God we have not seen (1 Jn 4.20)…[39]

In another place, he focuses the point in terms of Jesus Christ:

> Our neighbours are not concerned with our Christology, but they show from time to time, their interest in our 'neighborology.' Not 'you shall love the Lord your God with all your heart, and with all our soul, and with all your might' (Deut 6.5), but 'You shall love your neighbour as yourself' (Lev 19.18) will speak to them.[40]

This conviction yields all that is needed to begin to welcome strangers.

6   Questions to Consider

1 What are the important marks of your local context that shape your congregation's experience and understanding? In what ways are these things likely to impact response to asylum seekers?

2 How important is it to hear first-hand 'stories of exile'? How can your congregation encounter such testimony?

3 In what ways does the story of the flight into Egypt address your congregation? What connections do people make in response to preaching about it?

4 In what ways does your congregation's celebration of Christmas sentimentalise the biblical tradition? How might this be contested?

5 In what ways is your congregation 'local, outward-looking and participative'? Do any such ways suggest connection with asylum seekers?

6 How aware is your congregation of people of other faiths, and of their traditions? Does your congregation respond to people of other faiths in characteristic ways, and what might these mean for hospitality to asylum seekers?

7 Who belongs to your congregation's 'communion of saints'? Are there those who can assist and encourage you to welcome strangers?

8 What is your congregation's understanding and practice of holy communion? How does this affect the quality of your hospitality?

9 How does your congregation expect to encounter the presence of Christ? Is encounter with the needy seen as a means of grace?

Notes

1. Wider perspectives can be found in M Dummett, *On Asylum Seekers and Refugees* (London: Routledge, 2001).

2. I am grateful to readers of my draft text, David Clough and Greg Forster, for this and other helpful suggestions.

3. For other experiences see H Kimble, *Desperately Seeking Asylum* (Glasgow: Wild Goose, 1998) on Oxford; and B Thompson, *Shelter from the Storm:* (Peterborough: Epworth, 2003) on Manchester. I commend these books.

4. See A Biles, 'Rebranding Gateshead,' *Regeneration and Renewal* (March 15, 2002). For cautions about the notion of regeneration in the urban context, see R Furbey, 'Faith in Urban "Regeneration"?' *Modern Believing* 42 (2001), pp 5–15.

5. A Gormley, *Making An Angel* (London: Booth-Clibborn Editions, 1998).

6. Archbishop's Commission, *Faith in The City* (London: CHP, 1985).

7. See M Pacione (ed), *Britain's Cities* (London: Routledge, 1997); D Massey, J Allen and S Pile (eds), *City Worlds* (London: Routledge, 1999).

8. J Vincent, *Hope from the City* (Peterborough: Epworth, 2000).

9. A Harvey, *By What Authority?* (London: SCM, 2001) offers a vigorous defence of the consensus tradition. For an equally vigorous critique, see the excellent paper by H Wilmer, *Forms of Urban Mission* (Leeds: Leeds Church Institute, 2001).

10. I adopt the phrase 'believing, worshipping and belonging' from Colin Buchanan, as a useful measure of what religious affiliation may mean.

11. Refugee Council, *Changing Lives: Stories of Exile* (London: Refugee Council, 1997) pp 2, 7, 13, 15; see also A Bradstock and A Trotman (eds), *Asylum Voices* (London: CTBI, 2003).

12. Refugee Council, *My Name Came Up* (London: Refugee Council, 2000) p 41.

13. Other possibilities might have included the Exodus traditions of the Old Testament, and of course their centrality to the heart of the gospel, mapping on so many New Testament themes: Jesus' healing and table-fellowship, cross and resurrection, and so on; but in a congregation without a strong biblical knowledge-base, these avenues may have proved a distraction from practical action.

14. P Sharper and S Sharper (eds), *The Gospel in Art by the Peasants of Solentiname* (Maryknoll: Orbits, 1984) p 16.

15. Sharper and Sharper, *The Gospel in Art*, p 16.

16. Formerly the Evangelical Urban Training Project, whose work is concentrated on mission among those 'who can read, but don't.'

17. J I López Vigil and M López Vigil, *Just Jesus: The Passion Book* (New York: Crossroad, 2000) p 319.

18. López Vigil and López Vigil, *The Passion Book*, p 325.

19. M Stringer, 'Celebrating the Massacre of Innocence,' in K Reed and I Williston (eds), *Suffer the Little Children* (Birmingham: University of Birmingham, 2001) pp 143–156, p 153.

20 On urban questioning of the morality of God, see L Green, 'Blowing Bubbles: Poplar' in P Sedgwick (ed), *God in the City* (London: Mowbray, 1995) pp 72–92.

21 L Larson-Miller, 'Christmas Season,' P Fink (ed), *New Dictionary of Sacramental Worship* (Collegeville: Liturgical, 1991) pp 204–210, p 209.

22 S Boynton, 'The Liturgical Role of Children in Monastic Communities from the Central Middle Ages,' *Studio Liturgical* 28 (1998): pp 194–209.

23 Compare M Cotes, 'Standing in the Stable,' in H Walton and S Durbar (eds), *Silence in Heaven* (London: SCM, 1994) pp 4–8.

24 M Collins, 'Is the Adult Church Ready for Liturgy with Young Christians?' *Worship: Renewal to Practice* (Washington DC: Pastoral, 1987) pp 277–295, p 279.

25 Some reasons for the loss of focus on imagery of blood in understandings of atonement following experience of the Great War are explored in A Wilkinson, *The Church of England and the First World War* (London: SPCK, 1978) and *Dissent or Conform?* (London: SCM, 1986). In a very interesting essay, George Lindbeck notes decline in use of the imagery with proposals for vibrant alternative foci for contemporary doctrine of the atonement, G Lindbeck, 'Atonement and the Hermeneutics of Intratextual Social Embodiment,' in T R Philips and D L Oakholm (eds), *The Nature of Confession* (Downers Grove: IVP, 1996) pp 221–240.

26 This text taken from the *United Methodist Book of Worship* (Nashville: UMC, 1992) p 282.

27 I like this notion of biblical interpretation: see S C Barton, 'New Testament Interpretation as Performance' in *Life Together* (Edinburgh: T & T Clark, 2001) pp 223–250.

28 *Faith in the City*, chapter 4, *passim*; p 135.

29 For a very helpful essay along these lines see K Leech, 'Comfort or Transformation?' in *Subversive Orthodoxy* (Toronto: Anglican Book Centre, 1992) pp 33–55.

30 See M Collins, 'Critical Questions for Liturgical Theology,' *Worship: Renewal to Practice*, pp 115–132.

31 Here I consciously echo the four-fold action of Jesus at table: 'taking, blessing, breaking, given,' which may be at the centre of a sacramental spirituality. See D E Saliers, *Worship and Spirituality* (Akron: OSL, [2] 1996) pp 57–68.

32 Compare *Common Worship* (London: CHP, 2000) p 297.

33 See H Russell, *Local Strategic Partnerships* (Bristol: Policy Press, 2001).

34 I fear an approach to interfaith issues in which an amalgam of themes and concerns common to the religions is made central, to the exclusion of the particularities which give the religions their distinctness from each other. The approach invites the problem of not recognizing one's own religion in the amalgam. For a recent exploration of various perspectives, see A Race, *Interfaith Encounter* (London: SCM, 2001).

35 See S Ringe, 'A Gentile Woman's Story' in A Loades (ed), *Feminist Theology: A Reader* (London: SPCK, 1991) pp 49–57.

36 See an attractive elaboration of this point in D F Ford, *The Shape of Living* (London: Fount, 1997) chapter 1, *passim*.

37 See especially M Morse, *Kosake Koyoma* (Berlin: Lang, 1991).

38 K Koyoma, *Water Buffalo Theology* (Maryknoll: Orbis, 1999) p 150.

39 Koyoma, *Water Buffalo Theology*, pp 150–151.

40 Koyoma, *Water Buffalo Theology*, p 66.